DIRK MAIERHAFER

THE QUICK-START GUIDE TO FINANCIAL $UCCESS WORKBOOK

Stop Struggling and Start Winning with Money!

The Quick-Start Guide to Financial Success Workbook
© 2019 Dirk Maierhafer

Published by Privateering Press, an imprint of Insignis Interactive, Inc.

ISBN-13: 978-1-946730-11-4 (paperback)

Edited by Jennifer Harshman, HarshmanServices.com
Cover and Book Design by James Woosley, FreeAgentPress.com

X
PRIVATEERING PRESS

Published by Privateering Press
PrivateeringPress.com
Satsuma, Alabama 36572
VID: 20200808

AUTHOR'S NOTE

Life can be challenging. Especially when it comes to your financial life, *you can struggle* and try to figure it out on your own, *or* you can use a guide to get through them quickly.

The choice is yours.

TABLE OF CONTENTS

ABOUT THE AUTHOR

Dirk Maierhafer

DIRK MAIERHAFER HAS ALWAYS been a dollars-and-cents guy, looking for deals and ways to stretch a dollar just a little more. Not only has he done this for his own personal finances, he has also done this for his clients. As of April 2019, he has managed a little over 709 million dollars for his clients, many of whom constantly rank in the top 40 of Fortune 500 companies. He is continuously looking for more efficient and effective ways to save and stretch available funding. It is not always easy or popular, but when you only have a specific amount of dollars to work with—well, that is all you have to work with. On one specific occasion, he proposed a solution that would save tens of thousands of dollars and the government agency that was involved stated that no one has ever proposed such a creative solution to this issue before. At one point during his travels, he decided to jot down a few ideas on finances that would have been very helpful at different financial stages in his life.

Eventually, he thought, *What if I created a quick-reference guide to help make financial decisions that was easy to understand, easy to implement, and could be used at any point in a person's life? How many people could benefit from a guide like that? How many lives could be changed for the better? What kind of opportunities could this create? And most of all, how many dreams could be fulfilled?*

Out of those questions came *The Quick-Start Guide to Financial Success* and *The Quick-Start Guide to Financial Success Workbook.*

Mission Statement

My personal mission is to help you make better financial decisions throughout your life. Through easy-to-understand information and real-life examples, you will be able to reach your dreams faster than you ever thought possible, while having a better life than you could have imagined.

CHAPTER 1

Why Change?
The Normal Is Fine.

CHANGING THE WAY YOU normally go about making financial decisions can be difficult, but making small changes will make a huge difference throughout your journey.

Starting with the end in mind and working backward to figure out how you're going to start is the key. In other words, a goal, a target, or an objective is your end. Now you have to figure out how to get to where you want to be.

Let me ask you several questions to help jumpstart your thinking.

Are you happy with where you are financially? _____

What would you do if you had no major financial obligations?

_____

_____

_____

_____

_____

What do you dream of doing?

_____

_____

_____

_____

How are your current financial obligations holding you back?

_____

_____

_____

_____

What do you want to change to improve your financial situation?

_____

_____

_____

_____

What steps are you putting in place to change your spending habits?

_____

_____

_____

_____

What steps are you putting in place to change your saving habits?

_____

_____

_____

_____

_____

How do you plan to hold yourself accountable so you stay on track with your new saving and spending habits?

_____

_____

_____

_____

_____

What kind of plan do you have in place to make better financial choices each day?

_____

_____

_____

_____

_____

At what age do you want to retire? _____

With the retirement plan you currently have in place, will you have enough to retire at the age you want to retire? _____

What is your current plan to reach your retirement goal?

_____

_____

_____

_____

What adjustments do you need to make to reach your retirement goal?

_____

_____

_____

_____

At what age can you afford to retire? _____

Notes:

_____

_____

_____

_____

_____

CHAPTER 2

What's *Your* Definition
of Financial Success?

MOST OF US HAVE our own definition or vision of what financial success looks like, but most often we are influenced by what others may have, what friends or family may say, or by what the talking heads on TV are telling us what financial success looks like.

Stop! This is about *you*! This is about *your* definition or vision of financial success and no one else's! This means you need to be crystal clear on what financial success looks like to you. This could mean a specific dollar amount in the bank, a specific lifestyle you want to have, or a specific place you want to live by a certain age.

Document your current definition or vision of financial success on the next two pages. Later, you can revisit them, as they will change over time, and might change after you finish this workbook.

Current Date: _____

_____

_____

_____

_____

_____

_____

_____

_____

_____

_____

_____

_____

_____

_____

_____

_____

_____

_____

CHAPTER 3

History Will Repeat Itself, Repeat Itself, Repeat Itself. Will You?

A FEW FAMOUS SAYINGS COME to mind regarding history.

*"Those who don't know history
are destined to repeat it."*
—Edmund Burke (1729–1797)

*"Those who cannot remember the past
are condemned to repeat it."*
—George Santayana (1863–1952)

We tend to have very short memories these days, especially when things are going well or appear to be going well.

Let's start by reviewing what you're currently doing financially. This will allow you to see your spending patterns and make adjustments moving forward. Before we move forward, what do you think you are currently spending more of your money on—your needs or your wants?

Okay, let's see how good of a guesser you are. Let's start out by pulling your bank records for the last 3 months. You now need to review each item and mark it as an "N" for Need and a "W" for a Want.

After reviewing your bank statements, what have you found that you're actually spending more of your money on? Needs or Wants?

Are you starting to see your spending patterns? _____

What are your spending patterns?

_____

_____

_____

_____

_____

Let's look at these patterns a little deeper. What actions or emotions trigger you to spend or overspend?

_____

_____

_____

_____

_____

Being aware of your triggers will allow you to lessen or avoid them. What adjustments can you make to reduce the triggers that are causing you to fall into your spending patterns?

_____

_____

_____

_____

_____

Notes:

CHAPTER 4

Lack of Financial Education is By Design

"The number one problem in today's generation and economy is the lack of financial literacy."

—Alan Greenspan

IF YOU ARE SAVING, that's awesome. Keep it up, and bump it up! If not, it's time to start. Be intentional with your money. Know where your money is going and understand your financial specifics.

Money is the one thing we use on a daily basis, but in most cases, we have little to no education on how to use it in a way that will truly benefit us during our lifetime. Doesn't that seem a little crazy? We're able to put plans together for vacations, parties, business trips, meetings, and all sorts of other things in our lives, but when it comes to putting a plan together for our own money, we have a huge blind spot. This is where the lack of financial education starts to show up.

Thinking back to your childhood, do you remember when you learned how to use money and from whom? _____

Do you know how they learned how to use money? _____

Have you previously been taught how to use money correctly but you have lost your way? _____

Do you see another pattern forming? _____

What steps are you taking to improve your financial education?

_____

_____

_____

_____

_____

_____

How do you plan to pass along the financial information that you have gained to the next generation?

_____

_____

_____

_____

_____

_____

_____

Notes:

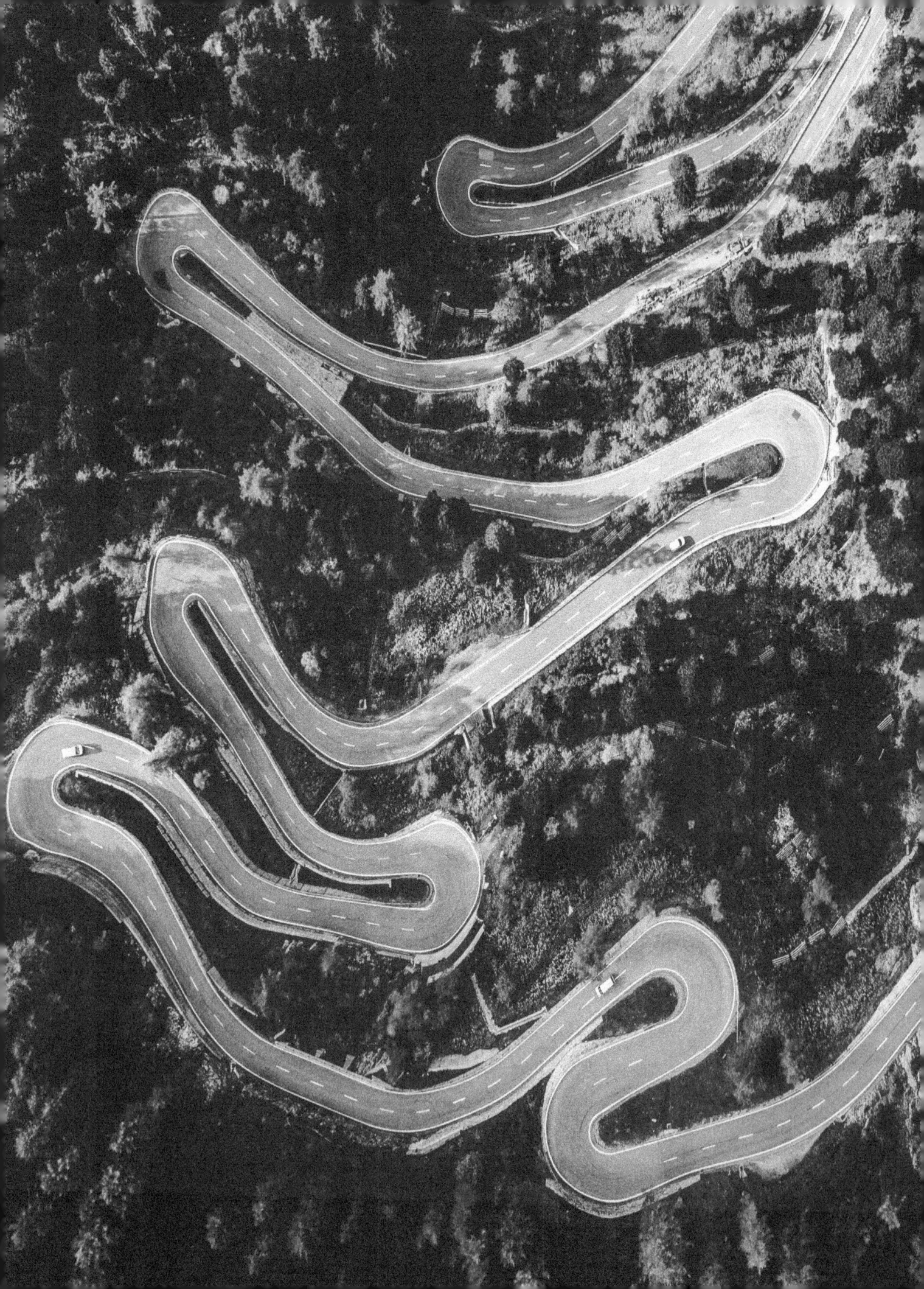

CHAPTER 5

The Journey to a Fatter Wallet

BUSINESSES USE BUDGETS TO control, track costs, and make sure they are going to be profitable. Makes sense, right? Wouldn't it make sense for *you* to also have a budget in order to control your costs and make sure you're profitable? Most of us try to leave work at work, but in some cases, we need to take what we have learned at work and apply it to our own lives to be successful..

Dirk says . . .

EACH OF US HAS 24 HOURS PER DAY—168 HOURS PER WEEK— 8,760 HOURS PER YEAR.
HOW WILL YOU SPEND YOUR TIME?

Are you ready to have a fatter wallet? _____

This will truly be a journey for you. It will be tough, and you will want to quit or take a break, but don't give up. Do it, and you will be so glad you hung in there once you're on the other side.

Are you ready to do this? _____

If so, let's get started.

You may think you're just trading dollars for stuff when you spend your money, but what you're actually doing is trading your future for stuff!

Dirk says . . .

COMMON PRACTICE DOES NOT EQUAL COMMON SENSE.

CHAPTER 6

A Winning Mindset

THE *OXFORD DICTIONARY* **DEFINES** mindset as, "The established set of attitudes held by someone."

In other words, your belief or approach about how you use money has formed over time, right or wrong. Well, I hate to be the bearer of bad news, but your mindset has been less than correct when it comes to money and how you can reach financial success. Let's take a look at what you know about money and how you can reach financial success.

It will take real effort on your part to change your way of thinking on how to use money, but it also takes patience and time. Have a plan in place that you can follow even if life is going great, but especially when life gets tough! Life happens!

On the lines below, make a list of what you can do with money.

_____

_____

_____

_____

_____

On the lines below, make a list of ways you can reach financial success.

_____

_____

_____

_____

_____

_____

Dirk Says . . .

WE ARE WHO WE CHOOSE TO BE
BY THE CHOICES WE MAKE,
SO CHOOSE WISELY.

Notes:

_____

_____

_____

_____

_____

_____

_____

_____

_____

_____

_____

_____

_____

_____

_____

_____

_____

_____

CHAPTER 7

What's Your Money Situation?

THIS IS AN IN-DEPTH view of your financial status. This should help clarify any misconceptions that you may have had about where you truly stand financially, and in most cases, it will scare the %&*@ out of you! The truth hurts, and sometimes it's not very pretty! By answering the questions in this chapter, you will have a better understanding of where you are financially. You can use this information to make the needed changes to become debt free, build wealth, reach your financial success, and have an awesome life.

WHY

Why don't you want to do a budget?

_____

_____

_____

_____

_____

_____

Why do you think a budget won't help you?

_____

_____

_____

_____

_____

Why do you not have an emergency fund?

_____

_____

_____

_____

_____

Why are you living paycheck to paycheck?

_____

_____

_____

_____

_____

Why are you going to change your spending and savings habits?

_____

_____

_____

_____

_____

_____

HOW

How often are you going to create and review your budget?

_____

_____

_____

_____

_____

How are you going to hold yourself accountable with the budget you have created?

_____

_____

_____

_____

_____

How are you going to change your spending and savings habits?

_____

_____

_____

_____

_____

How long will it be before you start your budget?

_____

_____

_____

_____

_____

How are you going to stick to your budget when you're on vacation?

_____

_____

_____

_____

_____

WHAT

What is stopping you from starting a budget today?

_____

_____

_____

_____

_____

_____

What are you going to change to stay on budget?

_____

_____

_____

_____

_____

_____

_____

Dirk says . . .

THE AVERAGE LIFE EXPECTANCY IS ABOUT 78 YEARS. THAT WORKS OUT TO 683,280 HOURS WITH A NORMAL 40-HOUR WORK WEEK. YOU WILL SPEND 35 YEARS OF THAT WORKING, OR 582,400 HOURS. DOES THIS PUT THINGS IN PERSPECTIVE?

STATUS

Are you living paycheck to paycheck?

_____

_____

Are you stressed out because you have more bills than money each month?

_____

_____

Are you and your significant other fighting about money?

_____

_____

What is your monthly take-home pay?

_____

_____

How much do you have in your savings?

_____

_____

Do you have $500–1,000 as a starter emergency fund?

_____

_____

Do you have back taxes you need to pay, if so, how much do you owe?

_____

Do you have any credit card bills? If so, how many credit card bills do you have?

_____

- *What is the current balance on each of your cards, and what is the combined total amount?*

_____

_____

_____

_____

_____

- *What are your monthly payments on each card, and what is the combined total amount?*

_____

_____

_____

_____

- *Do you pay them off every month? If not, what do you pay on them each month?*

_____

_____

_____

Do you have any car loans, and if so, how many loans do you have?

_____

- *What is the current balance on each car loan, and what is the combined total amount?*

    _____

    _____

    _____

- *What are your monthly payments on each, and what is the combined total amount?*

    _____

    _____

    _____

Do you have any miscellaneous loans (boat, ATV, RV, motorcycle, etc.), and if so, how many?

_____

- *What are the current balances on each, and what is the combined total amount?*

    _____

    _____

    _____

- *What are your monthly payments on each, and what is the combined total amount?*

    _____

    _____

    _____

Do you have student loans, and if so, how many do you have?

_____

- *Are they private, Federal, or both?*

  _____

- *What is the current balance on each student loan, and what is the combined total amount?*

  _____

  _____

  _____

- *What are your monthly payments on each student loan, and what is the combined total amount?*

  _____

  _____

  _____

Do you have a mortgage?

_____

- *Which type of loan is it? Conventional, FHA, VA, USDA rural housing, adjustable rate mortgage (ARM), 203k, or home equity line of credit (HELOC)?*

  _____

- *What is the current balance?*

  _____

- *What is your monthly payment?*

  _____

Do you have a second mortgage?

_____

- *Which type of loan is it? Conventional, FHA, VA, USDA rural housing, adjustable rate mortgage (ARM), 203k, or home equity line of credit (HELOC)?*

  _____

- *What is the current balance?*

  _____

- *What is your monthly payment?*

  _____

Do you pay rent, and if so, what is your monthly payment?

_____

_____

Do you pay child support, and if so, what is your monthly payment?

_____

_____

Do you pay alimony or palimony, and if so, what is the monthly payment?

_____

_____

Do you have collection agencies calling you?

_____

List the names of the collection agencies:

_____

_____

_____

- **What is the current balance of each amount owed?:**

  _____

  _____

- **What are your monthly payments on each amount owed?**

  _____

  _____

Notes:

_____

_____

_____

_____

_____

_____

_____

_____

CHAPTER 8

Hey! Where Did All My Money Go?
(Your Paycheck and Withholdings)

GETTING PAID IS WHAT it's all about. That's why you do what you do to get that cold hard cash in your hot little hands! Right? Today's that day; it's payday! You're adding up all the money in your head and dreaming of what you're going to do with all of it. The boss hands you that freshly sealed envelope with that little window in front with your name showing through it, and in your head, you start to hear MONEY, MONEY, MONEY, MOOONNNAAAAAAAAAAAAAY, MONNAAY . . . But all of a sudden, the needle scratches across the record and makes the most awful sound like fingernails across a chalkboard. The music stops . . . Hey! Where the heck is the rest of my money?

This will probably be a shock to those who are getting their first paycheck. Once you've accepted a job, normally on your first day you filled out a lot of paperwork, whether it was on real paper or online. You probably filled out medical, dental, retirement investing, life insurance, short-term disability (STD), and long-term disability (LTD) forms, along with state and Federal withholding forms (at least in the United States). A form called a W-4 or an Employee's Withholding Allowance Certificate is a Federal (IRS) form required to be filled out by all employees. This allows the employer to withhold a specific amount of money (income tax) based on your allowances as stated on the W-4 form. Your employer sends this directly to the IRS. This is the tax you owe to the Federal government (IRS) on the gross income you earned. States have their own specific withholding forms that are also required to be filled out, but some states do not have state income tax, so no form or withholdings are required at the state level.

Okay, get your paystub out and see where your money is going. If you get a refund each year, you will need to adjust your W-4 withholdings down so your employer is withholding less money from each of your paychecks. The opposite is true if you have to write a check to the IRS or the state each year.

Did you receive a refund last year from the IRS? _____

What was the amount of your IRS refund? $ _____

Did you receive a refund last year from your state? _____

What was the amount of your state refund? $ _____

Below, write in what your household is paying out in withholdings. This will allow you to see how much is being withheld from each paycheck. If you receive overtime, tips, or commissions, the amount will vary by paycheck, so only use your baseline income for this area.

	Income Source #1	Income Source #2	Household Total
Federal Taxes			
State Taxes			
Social Security			
Medicare			
Medical			
Dental			
LTD			
STD			
Retirement			
Vision			
Life Insurance			
Other:			
Other:			
Other:			
Other:			
TOTAL:			

Notes:

_____

_____

_____

_____

_____

_____

_____

_____

_____

_____

_____

_____

_____

_____

_____

_____

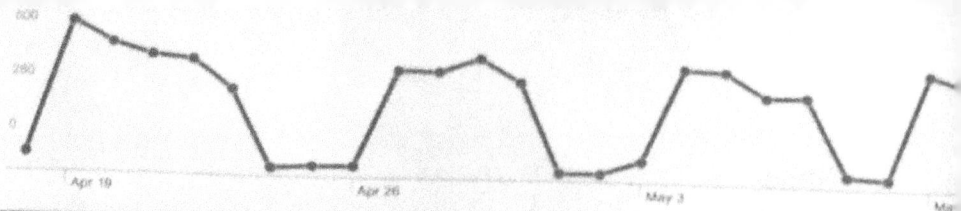

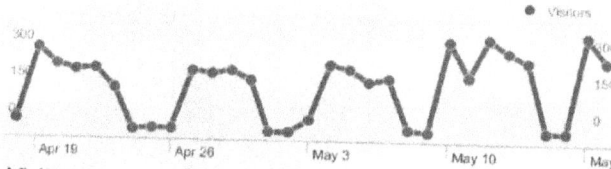

CHAPTER 9

Your Financial Scorecard

(Credit Reports, Credit Scores, and Identity Theft)

YOU ARE JUDGED FINANCIALLY by what is on your credit report and how high of a credit score you have. With a lower score, you could face higher insurance rates, higher interest rates on loans, outright denials for credit, or denial of job offers. Know what's on your credit report by pulling a free copy from each of the *three* major credit reporting agencies (Equifax, Experian, and TransUnion) from AnnualCreditReport.com. Know what's on your credit report, and know your credit score and dispute any errors, so your credit reports reflect your true financial history.

Freezing your credit is one of the best ways to combat identity theft.

Your score is generated by using algorithms that look at:

- Payment history (35%)
- Amount of debt owed (30%)
- Length of credit history (15%)
- New credit (10%)
- Types of credit used (10%)

Credit scores range from as low as 300 to as high as 850.

Do you know your credit score? _____

Have you pulled your credit report? _____

Have you disputed any inaccuracies that are listed on your credit report? _____

Are you paying your bills on time? _____

Do you have a large amount of debt compared to your income? _____

The banking industry views anything over a 36% debt to income ratio as being high. In my view (the only expert view that really matters in this workbook), anything over 0% is too high. You can't be financially success-ful if you're always giving your money to someone else!

Are you applying for new lines of credit to get the rewards? _____

Are you planning to buy a house soon? _____

If you are, your credit score will play a huge part in whether you are approved for a mortgage or not, so keep this in mind.

Have you frozen your credit with all three *major credit reporting agencies?* _____

Avoid Credit Monitoring Services—they can only alert you *after* something has happened!

Notes:

_____

_____

_____

_____

_____

_____

_____

_____

_____

_____

_____

_____

_____

_____

_____

_____

_____

_____

CHAPTER 10

Planning to Win

(Budgeting & Financial Strategy)

MONEY HAS MAGIC-LIKE QUALITIES—if you're not paying attention, it will just disappear. By actively planning where and how you're spending your money, you'll know where your money is going and why. How can you keep your money from disappearing, you may ask. By having a spending plan in place, that's how! In other words, a budget and a financial strategy.

If you don't have or follow a financial road map, you can't expect your money to stick around. You'll continue to struggle and always wonder where your money went.

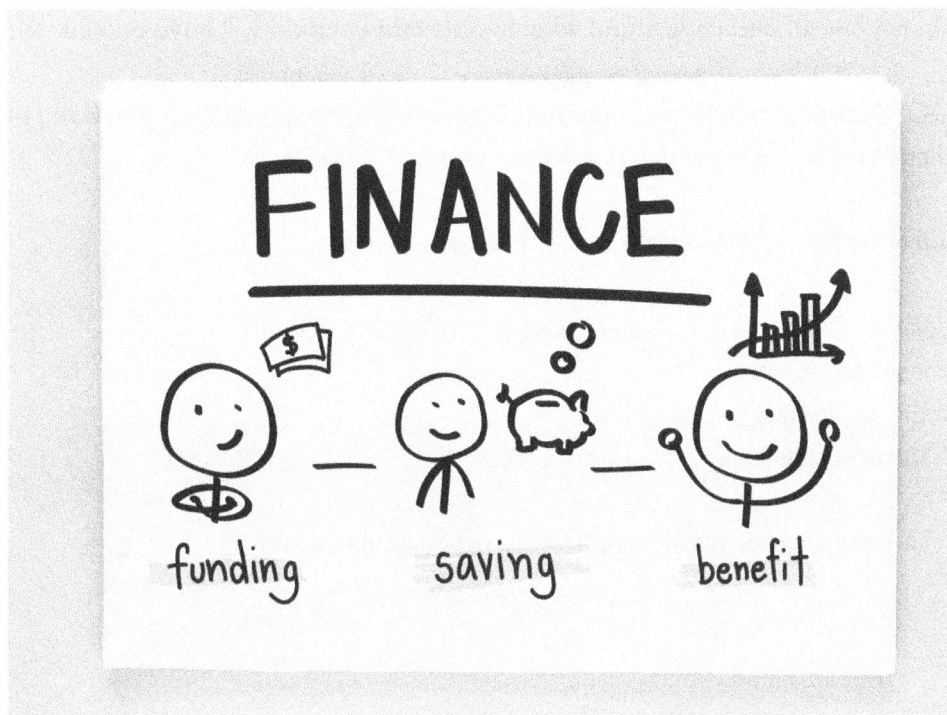

FINANCE

funding   saving   benefit

1. Financial awareness is #1. Being financially aware is understanding that almost everything you do will have some kind of financial impact on your budget.

2. Know the percentages on how much you should be spending in a given category.

   Typically, categories are broken down as follows:

   - Food (7–15%)
   - Housing (20–28%)
   - Utilities (5–10%)
   - Transportation (10%–15%)
   - Clothing (5%)
   - Savings (10–15%)
   - Medical (5–10%)
   - Personal (5–10%)
   - Entertainment (5–10%)
   - Debt (0–10%)
   - Giving (0–15%)

   Make sure your budget is in line with these percentages. These are recommended percentages. How high or low your take-home pay is will highly affect the percentages needed for the necessities.

3. Research before you buy. Be in the know. Don't impulse buy.

4. Avoid or step away from situations involving high pressure or high emotions when you're making a financial decision. You will most likely make a different choice when you have a chance to run the numbers yourself and understand what impact that decision will have on you financially.

5. The "COO" (Cash Only Option) is the best way to stop overspending. If you don't have the physical cash to buy something, guess what—you can't overspend!

Have you set up or do you already have a Starter Emergency Fund? _____

Which of the following options do you plan to use to eliminate your debt?
- ☐ **Debt consolidation loan**
- ☐ **Pay off the highest interest rates first**
- ☐ **Pay off the lowest balance first.**

How many of the Top 9 ways of getting out of debt are you going to use? _____

Notes:

_____

_____

_____

_____

_____

_____

_____

_____

_____

_____

_____

_____

_____

**The following pages are 12 months of my
Zero-Based Budget forms to help you keep on track.**

Head over to DirkWrites.com and sign up for the Inside Scoop!
Receive a FREE copy of this budget and a BONUS resource. Only those who sign up
will find out what the BONUS is and how it can help you with a huge financial decision.

Month 1: _____

HOUSEHOLD INCOME	
TOTAL BUDGET	
BALANCED BUDGET	

TOTAL SPENT SO FAR THIS MONTH	

WEEKLY TOTAL SPENT					
REMAINING CASH					

BUDGETED ITEMS	SPEND PLAN	$ SPENT Week 1	$ SPENT Week 2	$ SPENT Week 3	$ SPENT Week 4	$ SPENT Week 5	$ ACCUM	DIFFERENCE

EMERGENCY FUND RUNNING TOTAL			
3 Months	6 Months	9 Months	12 Months

COO = Cash Only Option

SAVING / INVESTING

Emergency Fund							
Savings							
Retirement Fund							
College Fund							
Investing							
Other							

HOUSING

1st Mortgage							
2nd Mortgage							
Property Tax							
Homeowner's / Renters Ins.							
Repairs / Maintenance							
Furnishings							
Other							

UTILITIES

Electricity							
Water							
Cell Phone							
Home Phone / Internet							
Trash							
Paid TV Service							
Other							
Other							

FOOD

Grocery (COO)							
Restaurants Family (COO)							
Restaurants Person 1 (COO)							
Restaurants Person 2 (COO)							
Other (COO)							
Other (COO)							

AUTO

Car Payment 1							
Car Payment 2							
Vehicle Insurance							
Gas / Oil (COO)							
Repairs / Tires / Maint. (COO)							
License / Taxes							
Vehicle Replacement							
Other							
Other							

CLOTHING

Adults (COO)							
Children (COO)							
Other (COO)							

MEDICAL / HEALTH

Health Ins / Doctor							
Dental Ins / Dentist							
Vision Ins / Optometrist							
Prescription / Vitamins							
Other (COO)							
Other (COO)							

PERSONAL

Life Insurance							
Disability Insurance							
Hair Care (COO)							
Toiletries / Cosmetics (COO)							
Gifts (Birthday / Christmas)							
School Tuition							
School Supplies							
Fun Time (COO)							
Donations (COO)							
Pet Care (COO)							
Other (COO)							
Other (COO)							

FUN STUFF

Entertainment (COO)							
Vacation							
Other (COO)							
Other (COO)							

DEBT

Debt Owed

						Debt Owed
Discover Card						
Master Card						
Visa						
American Express						
Dept. Store Card						
Other						
Other						
Other						
Other						
Other						

Budget Wins, Improvements, and Struggles:

Month 2: _____

HOUSEHOLD INCOME	
TOTAL BUDGET	
BALANCED BUDGET	

TOTAL SPENT SO FAR THIS MONTH	

WEEKLY TOTAL SPENT					
REMAINING CASH					

BUDGETED ITEMS	SPEND PLAN	$ SPENT Week 1	$ SPENT Week 2	$ SPENT Week 3	$ SPENT Week 4	$ SPENT Week 5	$ ACCUM	DIFFERENCE

EMERGENCY FUND RUNNING TOTAL			
3 Months	6 Months	9 Months	12 Months

COO = Cash Only Option

SAVING / INVESTING

Emergency Fund							
Savings							
Retirement Fund							
College Fund							
Investing							
Other							

HOUSING

1st Mortgage							
2nd Mortgage							
Property Tax							
Homeowner's / Renters Ins.							
Repairs / Maintenance							
Furnishings							
Other							

UTILITIES

Electricity							
Water							
Cell Phone							
Home Phone / Internet							
Trash							
Paid TV Service							
Other							
Other							

FOOD

Grocery (COO)							
Restaurants Family (COO)							
Restaurants Person 1 (COO)							
Restaurants Person 2 (COO)							
Other (COO)							
Other (COO)							

AUTO

Car Payment 1							
Car Payment 2							
Vehicle Insurance							
Gas / Oil (COO)							
Repairs / Tires / Maint. (COO)							
License / Taxes							
Vehicle Replacement							
Other							
Other							

CLOTHING

Adults (COO)							
Children (COO)							
Other (COO)							

MEDICAL / HEALTH

Health Ins / Doctor							
Dental Ins / Dentist							
Vision Ins / Optometrist							
Prescription / Vitamins							
Other (COO)							
Other (COO)							

PERSONAL

Life Insurance							
Disability Insurance							
Hair Care (COO)							
Toiletries / Cosmetics (COO)							
Gifts (Birthday / Christmas)							
School Tuition							
School Supplies							
Fun Time (COO)							
Donations (COO)							
Pet Care (COO)							
Other (COO)							
Other (COO)							

FUN STUFF

Entertainment (COO)							
Vacation							
Other (COO)							
Other (COO)							

DEBT

						Debt Owed
Discover Card						
Master Card						
Visa						
American Express						
Dept. Store Card						
Other						
Other						
Other						
Other						
Other						

Budget Wins, Improvements, and Struggles:

Month 3: _____

HOUSEHOLD INCOME	
TOTAL BUDGET	
BALANCED BUDGET	

TOTAL SPENT SO FAR THIS MONTH	

WEEKLY TOTAL SPENT					
REMAINING CASH					

BUDGETED ITEMS	SPEND PLAN	$ SPENT Week 1	$ SPENT Week 2	$ SPENT Week 3	$ SPENT Week 4	$ SPENT Week 5	$ ACCUM	DIFFERENCE

EMERGENCY FUND RUNNING TOTAL			
3 Months	6 Months	9 Months	12 Months

COO = Cash Only Option

SAVING / INVESTING

Emergency Fund								
Savings								
Retirement Fund								
College Fund								
Investing								
Other								

HOUSING

1st Mortgage								
2nd Mortgage								
Property Tax								
Homeowner's / Renters Ins.								
Repairs / Maintenance								
Furnishings								
Other								

UTILITIES

Electricity								
Water								
Cell Phone								
Home Phone / Internet								
Trash								
Paid TV Service								
Other								
Other								

FOOD

Grocery (COO)							
Restaurants Family (COO)							
Restaurants Person 1 (COO)							
Restaurants Person 2 (COO)							
Other (COO)							
Other (COO)							

AUTO

Car Payment 1							
Car Payment 2							
Vehicle Insurance							
Gas / Oil (COO)							
Repairs / Tires / Maint. (COO)							
License / Taxes							
Vehicle Replacement							
Other							
Other							

CLOTHING

Adults (COO)							
Children (COO)							
Other (COO)							

MEDICAL / HEALTH

Health Ins / Doctor							
Dental Ins / Dentist							
Vision Ins / Optometrist							
Prescription / Vitamins							
Other (COO)							
Other (COO)							

PERSONAL

Life Insurance							
Disability Insurance							
Hair Care (COO)							
Toiletries / Cosmetics (COO)							
Gifts (Birthday / Christmas)							
School Tuition							
School Supplies							
Fun Time (COO)							
Donations (COO)							
Pet Care (COO)							
Other (COO)							
Other (COO)							

FUN STUFF

Entertainment (COO)							
Vacation							
Other (COO)							
Other (COO)							

DEBT / Debt Owed

						Debt Owed
Discover Card						
Master Card						
Visa						
American Express						
Dept. Store Card						
Other						
Other						
Other						
Other						
Other						

Budget Wins, Improvements, and Struggles:

Month 4: _____

HOUSEHOLD INCOME	
TOTAL BUDGET	
BALANCED BUDGET	

TOTAL SPENT SO FAR THIS MONTH	

WEEKLY TOTAL SPENT					
REMAINING CASH					

BUDGETED ITEMS	SPEND PLAN	$ SPENT Week 1	$ SPENT Week 2	$ SPENT Week 3	$ SPENT Week 4	$ SPENT Week 5	$ ACCUM	DIFFERENCE

EMERGENCY FUND RUNNING TOTAL			
3 Months	6 Months	9 Months	12 Months

COO = Cash Only Option

SAVING / INVESTING

Emergency Fund							
Savings							
Retirement Fund							
College Fund							
Investing							
Other							

HOUSING

1st Mortgage							
2nd Mortgage							
Property Tax							
Homeowner's / Renters Ins.							
Repairs / Maintenance							
Furnishings							
Other							

UTILITIES

Electricity							
Water							
Cell Phone							
Home Phone / Internet							
Trash							
Paid TV Service							
Other							
Other							

FOOD

Grocery (COO)							
Restaurants Family (COO)							
Restaurants Person 1 (COO)							
Restaurants Person 2 (COO)							
Other (COO)							
Other (COO)							

AUTO

Car Payment 1							
Car Payment 2							
Vehicle Insurance							
Gas / Oil (COO)							
Repairs / Tires / Maint. (COO)							
License / Taxes							
Vehicle Replacement							
Other							
Other							

CLOTHING

Adults (COO)							
Children (COO)							
Other (COO)							

MEDICAL / HEALTH

Health Ins / Doctor							
Dental Ins / Dentist							
Vision Ins / Optometrist							
Prescription / Vitamins							
Other (COO)							
Other (COO)							

PERSONAL

Life Insurance							
Disability Insurance							
Hair Care (COO)							
Toiletries / Cosmetics (COO)							
Gifts (Birthday / Christmas)							
School Tuition							
School Supplies							
Fun Time (COO)							
Donations (COO)							
Pet Care (COO)							
Other (COO)							
Other (COO)							

FUN STUFF

Entertainment (COO)							
Vacation							
Other (COO)							
Other (COO)							

DEBT   Debt Owed

Discover Card						
Master Card						
Visa						
American Express						
Dept. Store Card						
Other						
Other						
Other						
Other						
Other						

Budget Wins, Improvements, and Struggles:

Month 5: _____

HOUSEHOLD INCOME	
TOTAL BUDGET	
BALANCED BUDGET	

TOTAL SPENT SO FAR THIS MONTH	

WEEKLY TOTAL SPENT					
REMAINING CASH					

BUDGETED ITEMS	SPEND PLAN	$ SPENT Week 1	$ SPENT Week 2	$ SPENT Week 3	$ SPENT Week 4	$ SPENT Week 5	$ ACCUM	DIFFERENCE

EMERGENCY FUND RUNNING TOTAL			
3 Months	6 Months	9 Months	12 Months

COO = Cash Only Option

SAVING / INVESTING

Emergency Fund							
Savings							
Retirement Fund							
College Fund							
Investing							
Other							

HOUSING

1st Mortgage							
2nd Mortgage							
Property Tax							
Homeowner's / Renters Ins.							
Repairs / Maintenance							
Furnishings							
Other							

UTILITIES

Electricity							
Water							
Cell Phone							
Home Phone / Internet							
Trash							
Paid TV Service							
Other							
Other							

FOOD

Grocery (COO)							
Restaurants Family (COO)							
Restaurants Person 1 (COO)							
Restaurants Person 2 (COO)							
Other (COO)							
Other (COO)							

AUTO

Car Payment 1							
Car Payment 2							
Vehicle Insurance							
Gas / Oil (COO)							
Repairs / Tires / Maint. (COO)							
License / Taxes							
Vehicle Replacement							
Other							
Other							

CLOTHING

Adults (COO)							
Children (COO)							
Other (COO)							

MEDICAL / HEALTH

Health Ins / Doctor							
Dental Ins / Dentist							
Vision Ins / Optometrist							
Prescription / Vitamins							
Other (COO)							
Other (COO)							

PERSONAL

Life Insurance							
Disability Insurance							
Hair Care (COO)							
Toiletries / Cosmetics (COO)							
Gifts (Birthday / Christmas)							
School Tuition							
School Supplies							
Fun Time (COO)							
Donations (COO)							
Pet Care (COO)							
Other (COO)							
Other (COO)							

FUN STUFF

Entertainment (COO)							
Vacation							
Other (COO)							
Other (COO)							

DEBT

						Debt Owed
Discover Card						
Master Card						
Visa						
American Express						
Dept. Store Card						
Other						
Other						
Other						
Other						
Other						

Budget Wins, Improvements, and Struggles:

Month 6: _____

HOUSEHOLD INCOME	
TOTAL BUDGET	
BALANCED BUDGET	

TOTAL SPENT SO FAR THIS MONTH	

WEEKLY TOTAL SPENT					
REMAINING CASH					

BUDGETED ITEMS	SPEND PLAN	$ SPENT Week 1	$ SPENT Week 2	$ SPENT Week 3	$ SPENT Week 4	$ SPENT Week 5	$ ACCUM	DIFFERENCE

EMERGENCY FUND RUNNING TOTAL			
3 Months	6 Months	9 Months	12 Months

COO = Cash Only Option

SAVING / INVESTING

Emergency Fund							
Savings							
Retirement Fund							
College Fund							
Investing							
Other							

HOUSING

1st Mortgage							
2nd Mortgage							
Property Tax							
Homeowner's / Renters Ins.							
Repairs / Maintenance							
Furnishings							
Other							

UTILITIES

Electricity							
Water							
Cell Phone							
Home Phone / Internet							
Trash							
Paid TV Service							
Other							
Other							

FOOD

Grocery (COO)							
Restaurants Family (COO)							
Restaurants Person 1 (COO)							
Restaurants Person 2 (COO)							
Other (COO)							
Other (COO)							

AUTO

Car Payment 1							
Car Payment 2							
Vehicle Insurance							
Gas / Oil (COO)							
Repairs / Tires / Maint. (COO)							
License / Taxes							
Vehicle Replacement							
Other							
Other							

CLOTHING

Adults (COO)							
Children (COO)							
Other (COO)							

MEDICAL / HEALTH

Health Ins / Doctor							
Dental Ins / Dentist							
Vision Ins / Optometrist							
Prescription / Vitamins							
Other (COO)							
Other (COO)							

PERSONAL

Life Insurance							
Disability Insurance							
Hair Care (COO)							
Toiletries / Cosmetics (COO)							
Gifts (Birthday / Christmas)							
School Tuition							
School Supplies							
Fun Time (COO)							
Donations (COO)							
Pet Care (COO)							
Other (COO)							
Other (COO)							

FUN STUFF

Entertainment (COO)							
Vacation							
Other (COO)							
Other (COO)							

DEBT / Debt Owed

Discover Card							
Master Card							
Visa							
American Express							
Dept. Store Card							
Other							
Other							
Other							
Other							
Other							

Budget Wins, Improvements, and Struggles:

Month 7: _____

HOUSEHOLD INCOME	
TOTAL BUDGET	
BALANCED BUDGET	

TOTAL SPENT SO FAR THIS MONTH	

WEEKLY TOTAL SPENT					
REMAINING CASH					

BUDGETED ITEMS	SPEND PLAN	$ SPENT Week 1	$ SPENT Week 2	$ SPENT Week 3	$ SPENT Week 4	$ SPENT Week 5	$ ACCUM	DIFFERENCE

EMERGENCY FUND RUNNING TOTAL			
3 Months	6 Months	9 Months	12 Months

COO = Cash Only Option

SAVING / INVESTING

Emergency Fund							
Savings							
Retirement Fund							
College Fund							
Investing							
Other							

HOUSING

1st Mortgage							
2nd Mortgage							
Property Tax							
Homeowner's / Renters Ins.							
Repairs / Maintenance							
Furnishings							
Other							

UTILITIES

Electricity							
Water							
Cell Phone							
Home Phone / Internet							
Trash							
Paid TV Service							
Other							
Other							

FOOD

Grocery (COO)							
Restaurants Family (COO)							
Restaurants Person 1 (COO)							
Restaurants Person 2 (COO)							
Other (COO)							
Other (COO)							

AUTO

Car Payment 1							
Car Payment 2							
Vehicle Insurance							
Gas / Oil (COO)							
Repairs / Tires / Maint. (COO)							
License / Taxes							
Vehicle Replacement							
Other							
Other							

CLOTHING

Adults (COO)							
Children (COO)							
Other (COO)							

MEDICAL / HEALTH

Health Ins / Doctor							
Dental Ins / Dentist							
Vision Ins / Optometrist							
Prescription / Vitamins							
Other (COO)							
Other (COO)							

PERSONAL

Life Insurance							
Disability Insurance							
Hair Care (COO)							
Toiletries / Cosmetics (COO)							
Gifts (Birthday / Christmas)							
School Tuition							
School Supplies							
Fun Time (COO)							
Donations (COO)							
Pet Care (COO)							
Other (COO)							
Other (COO)							

FUN STUFF

Entertainment (COO)							
Vacation							
Other (COO)							
Other (COO)							

DEBT / Debt Owed

						Debt Owed
Discover Card						
Master Card						
Visa						
American Express						
Dept. Store Card						
Other						
Other						
Other						
Other						
Other						

Budget Wins, Improvements, and Struggles:

Month 8: _____

HOUSEHOLD INCOME	
TOTAL BUDGET	
BALANCED BUDGET	

TOTAL SPENT SO FAR THIS MONTH	

WEEKLY TOTAL SPENT					
REMAINING CASH					

BUDGETED ITEMS	SPEND PLAN	$ SPENT Week 1	$ SPENT Week 2	$ SPENT Week 3	$ SPENT Week 4	$ SPENT Week 5	$ ACCUM	DIFFERENCE

EMERGENCY FUND RUNNING TOTAL			
3 Months	6 Months	9 Months	12 Months

COO = Cash Only Option

SAVING / INVESTING

Emergency Fund							
Savings							
Retirement Fund							
College Fund							
Investing							
Other							

HOUSING

1st Mortgage							
2nd Mortgage							
Property Tax							
Homeowner's / Renters Ins.							
Repairs / Maintenance							
Furnishings							
Other							

UTILITIES

Electricity							
Water							
Cell Phone							
Home Phone / Internet							
Trash							
Paid TV Service							
Other							
Other							

FOOD

Grocery (COO)							
Restaurants Family (COO)							
Restaurants Person 1 (COO)							
Restaurants Person 2 (COO)							
Other (COO)							
Other (COO)							

AUTO

Car Payment 1							
Car Payment 2							
Vehicle Insurance							
Gas / Oil (COO)							
Repairs / Tires / Maint. (COO)							
License / Taxes							
Vehicle Replacement							
Other							
Other							

CLOTHING

Adults (COO)							
Children (COO)							
Other (COO)							

MEDICAL / HEALTH

Health Ins / Doctor							
Dental Ins / Dentist							
Vision Ins / Optometrist							
Prescription / Vitamins							
Other (COO)							
Other (COO)							

PERSONAL

Life Insurance							
Disability Insurance							
Hair Care (COO)							
Toiletries / Cosmetics (COO)							
Gifts (Birthday / Christmas)							
School Tuition							
School Supplies							
Fun Time (COO)							
Donations (COO)							
Pet Care (COO)							
Other (COO)							
Other (COO)							

FUN STUFF

Entertainment (COO)							
Vacation							
Other (COO)							
Other (COO)							

DEBT

						Debt Owed
Discover Card						
Master Card						
Visa						
American Express						
Dept. Store Card						
Other						
Other						
Other						
Other						
Other						

Budget Wins, Improvements, and Struggles:

Month 9: _____

HOUSEHOLD INCOME	
TOTAL BUDGET	
BALANCED BUDGET	

TOTAL SPENT SO FAR THIS MONTH	

WEEKLY TOTAL SPENT					
REMAINING CASH					

BUDGETED ITEMS	SPEND PLAN	$ SPENT Week 1	$ SPENT Week 2	$ SPENT Week 3	$ SPENT Week 4	$ SPENT Week 5	$ ACCUM	DIFFERENCE

EMERGENCY FUND RUNNING TOTAL			
3 Months	6 Months	9 Months	12 Months

COO = Cash Only Option

SAVING / INVESTING

Emergency Fund							
Savings							
Retirement Fund							
College Fund							
Investing							
Other							

HOUSING

1st Mortgage							
2nd Mortgage							
Property Tax							
Homeowner's / Renters Ins.							
Repairs / Maintenance							
Furnishings							
Other							

UTILITIES

Electricity							
Water							
Cell Phone							
Home Phone / Internet							
Trash							
Paid TV Service							
Other							
Other							

FOOD

Grocery (COO)							
Restaurants Family (COO)							
Restaurants Person 1 (COO)							
Restaurants Person 2 (COO)							
Other (COO)							
Other (COO)							

AUTO

Car Payment 1							
Car Payment 2							
Vehicle Insurance							
Gas / Oil (COO)							
Repairs / Tires / Maint. (COO)							
License / Taxes							
Vehicle Replacement							
Other							
Other							

CLOTHING

Adults (COO)							
Children (COO)							
Other (COO)							

MEDICAL / HEALTH

Health Ins / Doctor							
Dental Ins / Dentist							
Vision Ins / Optometrist							
Prescription / Vitamins							
Other (COO)							
Other (COO)							

PERSONAL

Life Insurance							
Disability Insurance							
Hair Care (COO)							
Toiletries / Cosmetics (COO)							
Gifts (Birthday / Christmas)							
School Tuition							
School Supplies							
Fun Time (COO)							
Donations (COO)							
Pet Care (COO)							
Other (COO)							
Other (COO)							

FUN STUFF

Entertainment (COO)							
Vacation							
Other (COO)							
Other (COO)							

DEBT   Debt Owed

Discover Card							
Master Card							
Visa							
American Express							
Dept. Store Card							
Other							
Other							
Other							
Other							
Other							

Budget Wins, Improvements, and Struggles:

Month 10: _____

HOUSEHOLD INCOME					
TOTAL BUDGET			TOTAL SPENT SO FAR THIS MONTH		
BALANCED BUDGET					
WEEKLY TOTAL SPENT					
REMAINING CASH					

BUDGETED ITEMS	SPEND PLAN	$ SPENT Week 1	$ SPENT Week 2	$ SPENT Week 3	$ SPENT Week 4	$ SPENT Week 5	$ ACCUM	DIFFERENCE

EMERGENCY FUND RUNNING TOTAL			
3 Months	6 Months	9 Months	12 Months

COO = Cash Only Option

SAVING / INVESTING

Emergency Fund							
Savings							
Retirement Fund							
College Fund							
Investing							
Other							

HOUSING

1st Mortgage							
2nd Mortgage							
Property Tax							
Homeowner's / Renters Ins.							
Repairs / Maintenance							
Furnishings							
Other							

UTILITIES

Electricity							
Water							
Cell Phone							
Home Phone / Internet							
Trash							
Paid TV Service							
Other							
Other							

FOOD

Grocery (COO)							
Restaurants Family (COO)							
Restaurants Person 1 (COO)							
Restaurants Person 2 (COO)							
Other (COO)							
Other (COO)							

AUTO

Car Payment 1							
Car Payment 2							
Vehicle Insurance							
Gas / Oil (COO)							
Repairs / Tires / Maint. (COO)							
License / Taxes							
Vehicle Replacement							
Other							
Other							

CLOTHING

Adults (COO)							
Children (COO)							
Other (COO)							

MEDICAL / HEALTH

Health Ins / Doctor							
Dental Ins / Dentist							
Vision Ins / Optometrist							
Prescription / Vitamins							
Other (COO)							
Other (COO)							

PERSONAL

Life Insurance							
Disability Insurance							
Hair Care (COO)							
Toiletries / Cosmetics (COO)							
Gifts (Birthday / Christmas)							
School Tuition							
School Supplies							
Fun Time (COO)							
Donations (COO)							
Pet Care (COO)							
Other (COO)							
Other (COO)							

FUN STUFF

Entertainment (COO)							
Vacation							
Other (COO)							
Other (COO)							

DEBT / Debt Owed

						Debt Owed
Discover Card						
Master Card						
Visa						
American Express						
Dept. Store Card						
Other						
Other						
Other						
Other						
Other						

Budget Wins, Improvements, and Struggles:

Month 11: _____

HOUSEHOLD INCOME	
TOTAL BUDGET	
BALANCED BUDGET	

TOTAL SPENT SO FAR THIS MONTH					

WEEKLY TOTAL SPENT					
REMAINING CASH					

BUDGETED ITEMS	SPEND PLAN	$ SPENT Week 1	$ SPENT Week 2	$ SPENT Week 3	$ SPENT Week 4	$ SPENT Week 5	$ ACCUM	DIFFERENCE

EMERGENCY FUND RUNNING TOTAL			
3 Months	6 Months	9 Months	12 Months

COO = Cash Only Option

SAVING / INVESTING

Emergency Fund							
Savings							
Retirement Fund							
College Fund							
Investing							
Other							

HOUSING

1st Mortgage							
2nd Mortgage							
Property Tax							
Homeowner's / Renters Ins.							
Repairs / Maintenance							
Furnishings							
Other							

UTILITIES

Electricity							
Water							
Cell Phone							
Home Phone / Internet							
Trash							
Paid TV Service							
Other							
Other							

FOOD

Grocery (COO)							
Restaurants Family (COO)							
Restaurants Person 1 (COO)							
Restaurants Person 2 (COO)							
Other (COO)							
Other (COO)							

AUTO

Car Payment 1							
Car Payment 2							
Vehicle Insurance							
Gas / Oil (COO)							
Repairs / Tires / Maint. (COO)							
License / Taxes							
Vehicle Replacement							
Other							
Other							

CLOTHING

Adults (COO)							
Children (COO)							
Other (COO)							

MEDICAL / HEALTH

Health Ins / Doctor							
Dental Ins / Dentist							
Vision Ins / Optometrist							
Prescription / Vitamins							
Other (COO)							
Other (COO)							

PERSONAL

Life Insurance								
Disability Insurance								
Hair Care (COO)								
Toiletries / Cosmetics (COO)								
Gifts (Birthday / Christmas)								
School Tuition								
School Supplies								
Fun Time (COO)								
Donations (COO)								
Pet Care (COO)								
Other (COO)								
Other (COO)								

FUN STUFF

Entertainment (COO)								
Vacation								
Other (COO)								
Other (COO)								

DEBT / Debt Owed

Discover Card							
Master Card							
Visa							
American Express							
Dept. Store Card							
Other							
Other							
Other							
Other							
Other							

Budget Wins, Improvements, and Struggles:

Month 12: _____

HOUSEHOLD INCOME	
TOTAL BUDGET	
BALANCED BUDGET	

TOTAL SPENT SO FAR THIS MONTH	

WEEKLY TOTAL SPENT					
REMAINING CASH					

BUDGETED ITEMS	SPEND PLAN	$ SPENT Week 1	$ SPENT Week 2	$ SPENT Week 3	$ SPENT Week 4	$ SPENT Week 5	$ ACCUM	DIFFERENCE

EMERGENCY FUND RUNNING TOTAL			
3 Months	6 Months	9 Months	12 Months

COO = Cash Only Option

SAVING / INVESTING

Emergency Fund							
Savings							
Retirement Fund							
College Fund							
Investing							
Other							

HOUSING

1st Mortgage							
2nd Mortgage							
Property Tax							
Homeowner's / Renters Ins.							
Repairs / Maintenance							
Furnishings							
Other							

UTILITIES

Electricity							
Water							
Cell Phone							
Home Phone / Internet							
Trash							
Paid TV Service							
Other							
Other							

FOOD

Grocery (COO)							
Restaurants Family (COO)							
Restaurants Person 1 (COO)							
Restaurants Person 2 (COO)							
Other (COO)							
Other (COO)							

AUTO

Car Payment 1							
Car Payment 2							
Vehicle Insurance							
Gas / Oil (COO)							
Repairs / Tires / Maint. (COO)							
License / Taxes							
Vehicle Replacement							
Other							
Other							

CLOTHING

Adults (COO)							
Children (COO)							
Other (COO)							

MEDICAL / HEALTH

Health Ins / Doctor							
Dental Ins / Dentist							
Vision Ins / Optometrist							
Prescription / Vitamins							
Other (COO)							
Other (COO)							

PERSONAL

Life Insurance							
Disability Insurance							
Hair Care (COO)							
Toiletries / Cosmetics (COO)							
Gifts (Birthday / Christmas)							
School Tuition							
School Supplies							
Fun Time (COO)							
Donations (COO)							
Pet Care (COO)							
Other (COO)							
Other (COO)							

FUN STUFF

Entertainment (COO)							
Vacation							
Other (COO)							
Other (COO)							

DEBT   Debt Owed

Discover Card								
Master Card								
Visa								
American Express								
Dept. Store Card								
Other								
Other								
Other								
Other								
Other								

Budget Wins, Improvements, and Struggles:

CHAPTER 11

Quick and Easy Financial Wins

QUICK FINANCIAL WINS ARE both quick and easy—all it takes is a phone call. It's really that simple! Look at your cable bill, gasp, "That's how much I've been paying," and pick up the phone today! Remember it is your money, so why not keep as much of it as you can?

Call your service providers and ask them for a better deal. You can always reduce the service you have or cancel the service completely.

- ☐ **Land Line Provider**
- ☐ **Cell Phone Provider**
- ☐ **Cable Provider**
- ☐ **Internet Provider**
- ☐ **Paid TV Provider**
- ☐ **Streaming TV Provider**
- ☐ **Lawn Care Service**
- ☐ **Laundry Service**
- ☐ **Subscription Meal Kit Delivery Service**
- ☐ **Reoccurring Replenishment Services**
- ☐ **Car Insurance**
- ☐ **Renters Insurance**
- ☐ **Homeowners Insurance**
- ☐ **Other** _____
- ☐ **Other** _____
- ☐ **Other** _____
- ☐ **Other** _____

Notes:

_____

_____

_____

_____

_____

_____

_____

_____

CHAPTER 12

I'll Pay for That Later!
(Credit Cards)

**DANGER! DANGER! DANGER! DANGER! DANGER!
DANGER! DANGER! DANGER! DANGER! DANGER!**

Here's something to think about. If cash is king, why do you use plastic? Wow, that is a great question, if I do say so myself. Hopefully, you got the hint from the banner above that credit cards can be dangerous to your financial success.

1. First, find the APR listed on your statement. We will use 12% for this example.

2. Divide the APR by 365 (days in a year) to get your daily periodic rate (DPR). Credit cards charge interest *daily*, not annually, on an unpaid balance that is carried over to the next billing cycle.
   - 12% (APR) ÷ 365 (days per year) =.00032(DPR)

3. Calculate your average daily balance (ADB) over a billing cycle. We're going to use a 30-day billing cycle for this example. Say you start November 1 with an $1,800 unpaid balance from the previous billing cycle. Then on November 16, you make an $800 payment, leaving an unpaid balance of $1,000 for the remainder of the billing cycle ending on November 30. You will need to add up each of the daily balances for the entire billing cycle to find the sum of your daily balances.
   - $1,800 × 15 Days = $27,000 (ADB)
   - $1,000 × 15 Days = $15,000 (ADB)
   - $27,000 + $15,000 = $42,000 (SUM of daily balances)
   - $42,000 ÷ 30 Days = $1,400 (ADB) for the month

4. Calculate what the interest will be by using the Average Daily Balance × Daily Periodic Rate × Days in the billing cycle.
   - $1,400 (ADB) × .00032(DPR) × 30 Days = $13.44 of interest

You will be charged $13.44 of interest on that unpaid balance. However, because interest is calculated daily, your balance will continue to rise every day until a payment is made or the balance is paid off.

Dirk says . . .

IF CASH IS KING,
WHY DO YOU USE PLASTIC?

Use the area below to figure out the interest you will be paying as of today.

Credit Card #1

_____% APR

_____% (APR) ÷ 365 (days per year) =._____ (DPR)

_____ × _____ Days = $_____ (ADB)

$_____ × _____ Days = $_____ (ADB)

$_____ + $_____ = $_____ (SUM of daily balances)

$_____ ÷ _____ Days = $_____ (ADB) for the month

$_____ (ADB) × _____ (DPR) × _____ Days = $_____ of interest

Credit Card #2

_____% APR

_____% (APR) ÷ 365 (days per year) =._____ (DPR)

_____ × _____ Days = $_____ (ADB)

$_____ × _____ Days = $_____ (ADB)

$_____ + $_____ = $_____ (SUM of daily balances)

$_____ ÷ _____ Days = $_____ (ADB) for the month

$_____ (ADB) × _____ (DPR) × _____ Days = $_____ of interest

Credit Card #3

_____% APR

_____% (APR) ÷ 365 (days per year) =._____ (DPR)

_____ × _____ Days = $_____ (ADB)

$_____ × _____ Days = $_____ (ADB)

$_____ + $_____ = $_____ (SUM of daily balances)

$_____ ÷ _____ Days = $_____ (ADB) for the month

$_____ (ADB) × _____ (DPR) × _____ Days = $_____ of interest

Credit Card #4

_____% APR

_____% (APR) ÷ 365 (days per year) =._____ (DPR)

_____ × _____ Days = $_____ (ADB)

$_____ × _____ Days = $_____ (ADB)

$_____ + $_____ = $_____ (SUM of daily balances)

$_____ ÷ _____ Days = $_____ (ADB) for the month

$_____ (ADB) × _____ (DPR) × _____ Days = $_____ of interest

Dirk says . . .

LIFE IS A SERIES OF TRADE-OFFS. YOU TRADE YOUR TIME FOR MONEY. YOU TRADE YOUR MONEY FOR THINGS. ARE YOU TRADING YOUR FUTURE FOR THE PRESENT, WHEN YOU SHOULD BE TRADING YOUR PRESENT FOR YOUR FUTURE?

Credit Card #5

_____% APR

_____% (APR) ÷ 365 (days per year) =._____ (DPR)

_____ × _____ Days = $_____ (ADB)

$_____ × _____ Days = $_____ (ADB)

$_____ + $_____ = $_____ (SUM of daily balances)

$_____ ÷ _____ Days = $_____ (ADB) for the month

$_____ (ADB) × _____ (DPR) × _____ Days = $_____ of interest

Self-control and discipline are two characteristics that you must have if you're planning on having and using a credit card. Without them, you will end up like most of the people around you: all flash, no cash, living from paycheck to paycheck month after month, year after year, always struggling to make ends meet, always wondering why you can't get ahead. You can also look forward to being stressed out for months, years, or even decades. That doesn't sound like so much fun, does it?

Notes:

_____

_____

_____

_____

_____

_____

_____

_____

CHAPTER 13

I Can't Drive 55!

(Car Insurance and Buying That New Ride)

A SURPRISING COST THAT IS normally an afterthought is car insurance. This book is a little different. I want to challenge you to think differently about your financial decisions. That's why you need to look at car insurance *before* you buy a car, not after. Research how much the insurance is going to cost you as well as which kinds of coverages you will need for the type of vehicle your thinking about buying. In most cases, you're going to be surprised and not in a good way at how much it's going to cost you to insure your dream vehicle. By looking at your insurance costs first, you may change your mind on which kind of vehicle you're going to buy. I can't imagine how much money I could have saved if I would have known about this little life hack before I bought my first car.

Keeping That Ride Safe

What are you currently paying for car insurance? $_____

Let's see if you can keep a little more of your hard earned money. List the car insurance companies you are going to contact for a car insurance quote. Remember, you need at least three quotes to compare against your existing car insurance.

_____

_____

_____

Review each of the quotes. If you have any questions, call the insurance company that you received the quote from to ask for clarifications until you understand their coverages.

Do all of the quotes have the same coverage? _____

If not, what are the pros and cons of each?

Pros

_____

_____

_____

_____

Cons

_____

_____

_____

_____

What are your premiums going to be, based on? (Remember, the lowest quote may not be the best quote.)

Normally, you will save money if you pay for longer durations up front. If you pay for your vehicle insurance monthly, you will typically be charged a service fee because you did not pay for the insurance in full.

Car Insurance Payment Breakdown

- ***Per Month: $_____***

- ***Per Quarter: $_____   Per Month: $_____***

- ***Per 6 Months: $_____   Per Month: $_____***

- ***Per Year: $_____   Per Month: $_____***

Buying That New Ride

Buying New

Avoid buying a brand-new vehicle as it will cost you a lot of money upfront and quickly goes down in value. That huge car payment you're going to be making each month can be used for building your wealth instead of reducing it. I know, I know, it's all shiny and new and it has that new-car smell. But don't, just don't.

Buying Used

Buying a used vehicle is your next and best option (unless of course someone gives you a vehicle). Plain and simple, buying a used vehicle will save you a lot of money! As you can see from above, *the value of a new vehicle drops significantly over 5 years*. Buying a used vehicle eliminates a lot of that loss and will keep more money in your pocket. The great news is that vehicle reliability has improved dramatically over the years, and vehicles are on the road a lot longer than they used to be.

Lease a Vehicle

Leasing is basically renting, and you're paying a premium to do this. You will have all of the responsibility and obligation with none of the benefits. Avoid this option as well.

Extended Warranties

If you want an extended warranty, only buy the manufacturer's extended warranty, as 3rd-party warranty companies may just close up shop and leave you with nothing except an empty wallet.

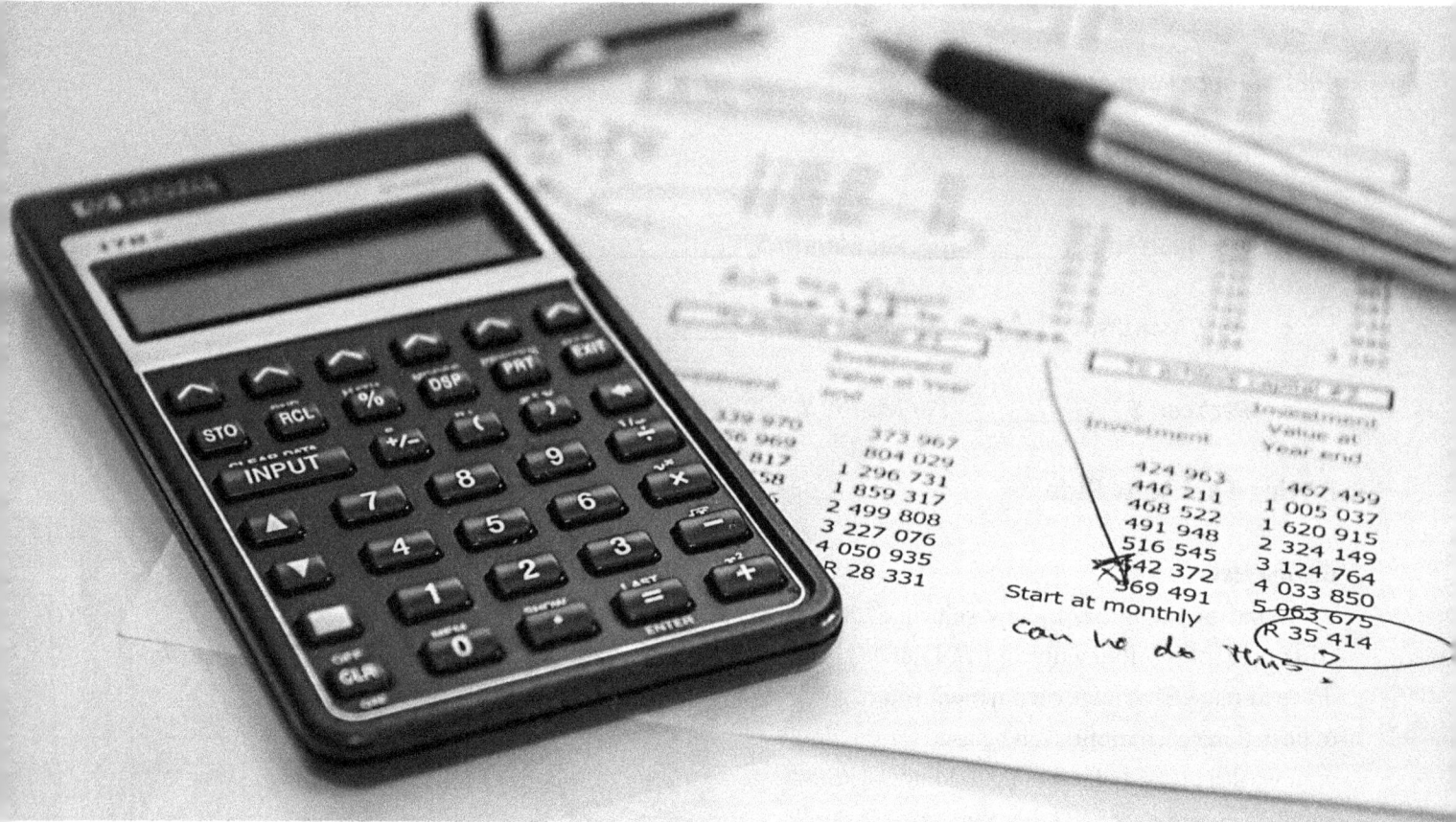

What amount of money are you willing to spend on a vehicle? $_____

How much money do you have saved for that "new to you" vehicle? $_____

Do you plan to pay cash for the vehicle? _____

If not, why not? _____

Do you plan to take out a loan for the vehicle? _____ *(Why? That's a broke person's way of thinking.)*

If so, what is the duration of the loan (it needs to be for less than 42 months)? _____

Do you at least have a sizable down payment? _____

If so, what amount are you putting down? $_____

Have you done your research on the vehicle? _____

What has the research revealed?

_____

_____

_____

_____

_____

_____

_____

Have you set up your test drive? _____

Do you have a vehicle inspection set up? _____

Have you verified that the person or company you are going to take the vehicle to for inspection is reputable? _____

Dirk says . . .

IF YOU'RE IN DEBT, YOU'RE TRADING FUTURE OPPORTUNITIES FOR FEEL-GOOD MOMENTS RIGHT NOW.

Notes:

_____

_____

_____

Glass

GLASS

FRA GILE

FRAGI

FRAG

Computer

CHINA Chin

ILE

FRA

Kitchen

Kitchen

To

itchen

fragile

FRAGI

CHAPTER 14

A Temporary Situation
(Moving, Renters Insurance, and Renting Basics)

MOVING CAN BE BOTH exciting and daunting at the same time. It can also be a costly endeavor by itself, and you need to be aware of the moving scams that are out there.

Have you confirmed whether or not your renters or homeowners insurance policy includes moving insurance? _____

If not, federal law mandates that moving companies offer at least two types of coverage: Full Value Protection and Released Value Protection.

Before Moving In

Have you set up a date and time with the landlord to walk through the property you plan to rent? _____

Are you ready to document with video and/or photos any existing issues the property may have before signing the rental agreement? _____

Read and understand your rental agreement before you sign it! In fact, ask if you can have a copy of the agreement 3 days before signing, as this will give you time to read the contract in its entirety.

Before Moving Out

Are you prepared to move out and get your security deposit back? _____

Did you clean the dwelling from top to bottom? _____

Did you repair any damage you may have caused? _____

Did you clean the carpets? _____

Have you set up a date and time with the landlord to walk through the rental property before you move out? _____

Are you ready to document with video and/or photos the conditions in which you are leaving the rental property? _____

Notes:

_____

_____

_____

CHAPTER 15

College Knowledge

Warning!

THIS CHAPTER CAN CHANGE your life! I know, this is a bold statement, but it's a true statement nevertheless.

Having the Knowledge to Pick the Right College

This is a huge decision that will change your life. You absolutely must pick the right college! You need to choose a college that is *right for you*.

Top 12 items to consider when choosing a college

1. Cost
2. Degree/Major availability
3. Campus size
4. Student life
5. Student body diversity
6. Current students' opinions of the college
7. What the college is really focused on
8. Student–Teacher ratio
9. Location
10. On-Campus housing options
11. Graduating data
12. School rankings

The best way to pay for your higher education is to have someone else pay for it! This can be done through scholarships, grants, joining the military, or even having your employer pay for it. If you have to pay out of pocket, pay-as-you-go is the next best way to pay for your higher education. If you take out a loan, you only want to take out a Federal loan, such as the Stafford loan, and avoid all private loans. Keeping your cost low is key.

Avoid overpaying for your college education!

Have you started looking for ways to pay for college? _____

What steps have you taken to figure out how you are going to pay for college?

_____

_____

_____

_____

_____

_____

_____

Have you looked for educational scholarships? _____

If so, have you made a list of possibilities? _____

If not, you need to make one.

_____

_____

_____

_____

_____

_____

_____

Have you looked for educational grants? _____

If so, have you made a list of possibilities? _____

If not, you need to make one.

_____

_____

_____

_____

_____

_____

_____

Are you considering joining the military? _____

If so, have you interviewed recruiters from each branch to see which one may best fit your needs? _____

If not, this would be your first step.

When choosing a college, start early and take your time. Make sure the college you want to go to will be a good fit for you. This is a huge decision that will change your life. You absolutely must pick the right college! You need to choose a college that is right for you.

By answering the following questions, you will gain a better understanding of who you are and how that can help you in the future. This should help you focus on what kind of career path you would enjoy and what kind of college would best fit your needs.

What do you do for fun?

_____

_____

_____

_____

What kind of activities pique your interests?

_____

_____

_____

What do you enjoy doing that you could do for hours on end?

_____

_____

_____

Do you enjoy being indoors or outdoors? _____

Do you enjoy being active or less active? _____

Are you a people person or someone who likes to be behind the scenes? _____

It's important to do what you enjoy doing!

Notes:

_____

_____

_____

_____

_____

_____

_____

CHAPTER 16

Walking Down the Aisle

WEDDINGS CAN BE VERY expensive! Be in agreement on what your needs and wants are for your wedding. Search for creative ways to have an awesome wedding without breaking your piggy bank. The wedding is about you and your soon-to-be spouse, not anyone else.

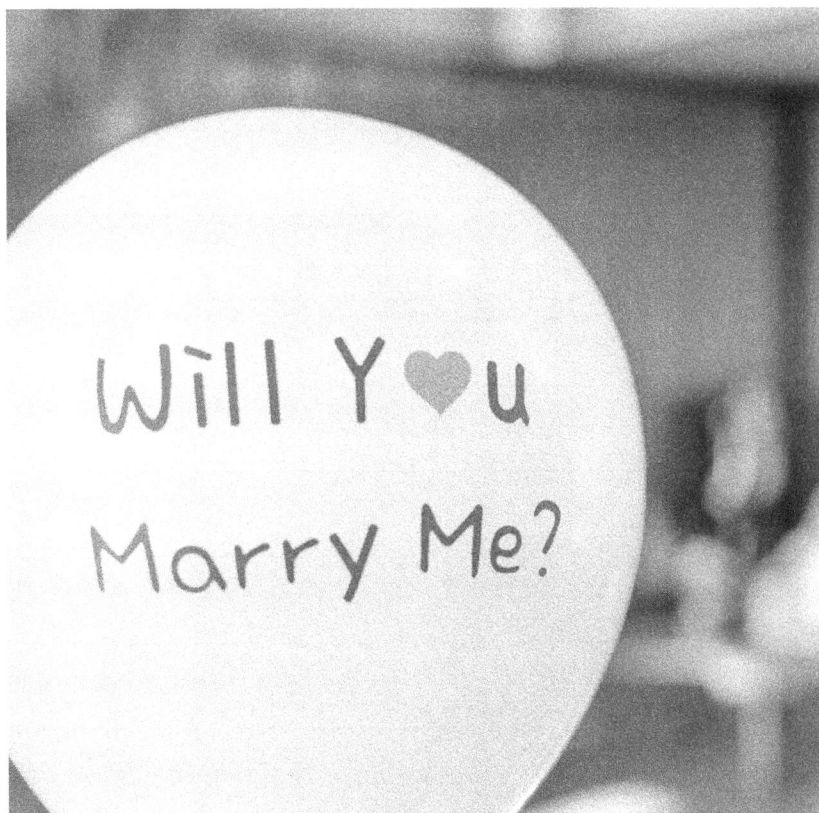

Needs

_____

_____

_____

_____

_____

_____

_____

_____

_____

_____

_____

_____

_____

_____

_____

_____

_____

_____

Wants

_____

_____

_____

_____

_____

_____

_____

_____

_____

_____

_____

_____

_____

_____

_____

_____

_____

Notes:

_____

_____

_____

_____

_____

_____

_____

_____

_____

_____

_____

_____

_____

_____

_____

_____

_____

CHAPTER 17

To Will or Not to Will, That is the Question

MAKING A GREAT FINANCIAL decision can last for years and years, even if you're not around. Taking care of your family should be your first priority. A will can help you do that, but most of us just don't get around to creating one. I don't see that as being acceptable; do you? So, why not make sure that your family is taken care of by having the last word in writing?

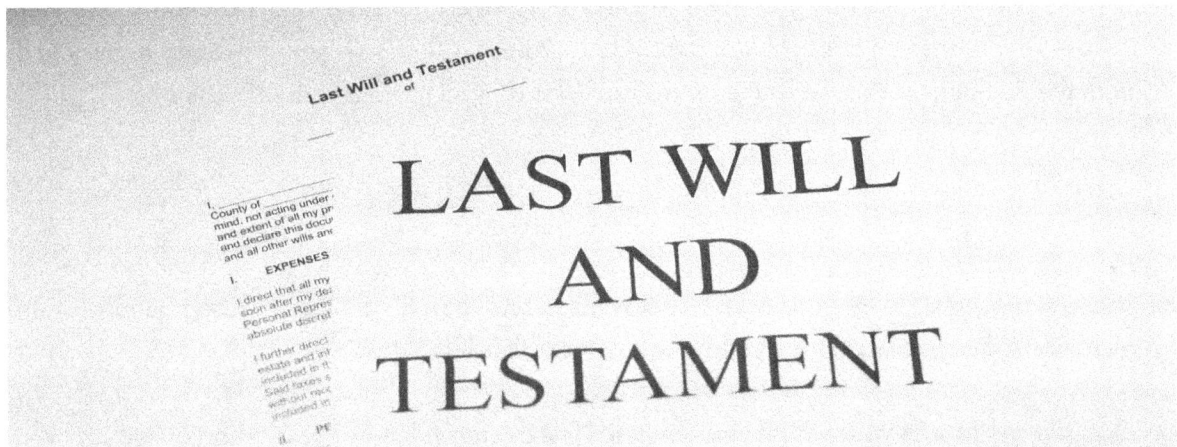

Don't know where to start? Here are a few items to keep in mind.

1. You can write your own will, use an online service, or have a lawyer draft a will for you. Laws differ depending on where you live, so you may need to contact your state government for more details. What option will work best for you?
   - ☐ Write your own will?
   - ☐ Use an online service?
   - ☐ Have a lawyer draft a will for you?

2. You will need to appoint someone who can carry out your wishes per your will. The person is called an executor. You need to officially state who is going to be your executor, but you need to make sure they are willing and able to do so. You also need to choose an alternate executor as a backup plan.
   - Original executor _____
   - Alternate executor _____

3. List your heirs or beneficiaries. These don't necessarily have to be family members, but laws may differ depending on where you live, so be sure to confirm this with a legal professional if you list non-family members.

   _____

   _____

   _____

4. If you have minor children, you will also need to name a guardian. This is someone who will follow your wishes on how you want them to be raised. Of course, you will need to discuss this with the person you choose as the guardian. Who do you currently have in mind?

   _____

5. You will also need to list your assets, assess them, and then divide them among beneficiaries as you see fit. Be specific on how your assets will be divided.

6. Don't forget to sign your will! If you don't, it's just a letter telling people who you would like to get your assets, but it's not legally binding. In some cases, you will also need to get your will notarized.

7. Depending on where you live, you may also need to have multiple witnesses sign your will to make it a legal document.

Notes:

CHAPTER 18

Kids Are
Really Expensive!

FROM ALL THE RESEARCH I have done and from what I have heard experts say, kids are expensive! Plan on spending a lot of money if you are planning on having one. As with anything, depending on which part of the country you live in—heck, even which part of the city you live in—costs can vary tremendously.

The good thing is that you can use the budget from Chapter 10 to help plan well in advance of having kids! This way you won't have to stress out (at least not financially) when the news comes: "We're pregnant!"

List the items that you are most concerned about now that you have a child on the way.

_____

_____

_____

_____

_____

List the ideas that you have and that you can put in to place to minimize or eliminate those concerns.

_____

_____

_____

_____

_____

Notes:

_____

_____

_____

_____

_____

_____

CHAPTER 19

My Home is My Castle
(Insuring, Funding, and Picking the Right Home for You)

HOMEOWNERS INSURANCE IS A policy that covers losses and damages as well as assets within the home. It also provides liability coverage against accidents in the home or on the property. Homeowners insurance can vary greatly in cost due to a multitude of factors such as location, size of house, type of pets, number of previous claims, amount of coverage, and the insurance company itself.

Has your property changed in value since you purchased your home? _____

Has the cost of your insurance gone up along with your home value? _____

If not, it should have. Your insurance company should be raising your premium to keep up with the increase of your home value. If it's worth more, it will cost more to repair your home.

Who do you currently have your homeowners policy with? _____

When was the last time you comparison shopped for a homeowners policy? _____

If not recently, you need to. When will you make this happen? _____

List the homeowners insurance companies you are going to contact for a quote. You need at least three.

_____

_____

_____

_____

_____

What are your premiums going to be, based on the quotes (remember, the lowest quote may not be the best quote)?

Normally, you will save money if you pay for longer durations up front. If you pay for your homeowners insurance monthly, you will typically be charged a service fee because you did not pay for the insurance in full.

Homeowners Insurance Payment Breakdown

- *Per Month: $_____*

- *Per Quarter: $_____ / Per Month: $_____*

- *Per 6 Months: $_____ / Per Month: $_____*

- *Per Year: $_____ / Per Month: $_____*

First-time home buyers

The best advice I can give you here is to try to be debt free before buying your first home! I, like most of you, heard from the people around me that you need to buy a house and stop wasting your money on rent. Let's do a little translation here. *You have people who are broke telling you how to be broke just like them.* Is that really a smart move?

When possible, save and pay cash for your first house. If you're not willing to wait, make sure you have a huge down payment before thinking about getting a mortgage.

A 15-year, fixed-rate mortgage is the longest mortgage you should take out; otherwise, you cannot afford the house you want to purchase. If you take out a mortgage, keep it simple. Do not take out an atypical mortgage to get that house, because in the end, it will most likely cause you a headache.

How much have you saved for your down payment? $_____

What kind of loan are you looking for?
- [ ] **Conventional**
- [ ] **FHA**
- [ ] **VA**
- [ ] **USDA Rural Housing**
- [ ] **Adjustable-rate mortgage (ARM)**
- [ ] **203k**
- [ ] **HELOC (home equity line of credit)?**

Have you comparison shopped for your mortgage with at least 3 lenders? _____

- *Avoid the big banks. Try credit unions and smaller community banks when looking for an initial mortgage. Online offers are usually the best way to refinance an existing mortgage, but not necessarily for an initial mortgage. It's always nice when you can sit down and go over the paperwork with someone in person that does this day in and day out versus, trying to do this over the phone with someone in a far off land many, many states away.*

Which credit unions and smaller community banks are in your area?

_____

_____

Have you chosen a title company to use? _____

How much do you have saved for your closing costs? $_____

Have you scheduled the final walk-through of the property before you sign the mortgage paperwork? _____

Review the mortgage paperwork and ensure that all the items you noted during the walk-through and that were agreed to be fixed are listed in the contract. If they are not, they will not be fixed.

When you are in the process of choosing a house, do not exceed your budget, and do not let your emotions make the choice for you. You do not want to end up regretting it every month when you make your mortgage payment, do you? Use the How to Choose a House Checklist to help you narrow down your needs and wants. Look at lots and lots of houses online to help dial in your needs to a specific area. Look for a qualified full-time real estate agent that has ten years of experience, has sold at least 200 houses, and specializes in the area you are interested in.

Keep in mind the obligations that come with being a homeowner.

- Earnest money
- Down payment
- Closing costs
- Mortgage insurance
- Homeowners insurance
- HOA dues (homeowners' association)
- Property taxes
- Appliances
- Furnishings
- Maintenance, and so on

Notes:

_____

_____

_____

_____

_____

_____

_____

_____

_____

_____

_____

_____

_____

_____

The How to Choose a House Checklist is a great tool to narrow down what type of home best fits you, your needs, and your wants.

How to Choose a House Checklist

Budget: $_____

LOCATION

	Need	Want	N/A		Need	Want	N/A
Urban Location				Rural Location			

SPECIFIC LOCATION

Quiet or Secluded				Walking or Golf Cart Community			
Lake/Ocean View				Cul-de-Sac			
Mountain View				The Heart of the City			
City Skyline View				Nice Suburban Neighborhood			

ITEMS TO CONSIDER BASED ON LOCATION

Min. Distance to Work ____				New Neighborhood			
Max. Commute Time to Work ____				Established Neighborhood			
Emergency Service Response Times				Gated Community			
Cell Service Reliability				Limited Building Access (Security)			
Utility Reliability (Power, Water, Gas, Sewer)				Access to Top-Ranked Public Schools			
Min. Distance to Grocery and Retail Stores ____				Access to Top-Ranked Private Schools			
Access to Public Transportation				Parks, Green Space, or Dog Parks			

HOUSE SPECIFICS

Min. Age of the Home ____				Crawl Space (Open)			
Max. Age of the Home ____				Crawl Space (Sealed)			
Min. Sq. Footage of the Home ____				Basement			
# of Story Home ____				Private Garage			
Min. Age of the Roof ____				Min. # Car Garage ____			
Attic Space Built for Storage				Parking Structure			
Max. Age of the HVAC System ____				Street Parking			
Max. Age of the Water Heater ____							

HEATING AND A/C (Common Heating Options: Electric / Natural Gas / Propane / Solar / Wood / Fuel Oil / Steam)

Energy Efficient				Heat Pump			
Central Heating and Air				Boiler			
Fireplace				Electric Baseboard Heater			
Wood Stove/Pellet Stove							

EXTERIOR

Low Maintenance Exterior					Deck			
Large Yard (Fenced-In)					Patio			
Large Yard					Pool			
Small or No Yard					Sunroom			
Porch					Outside Storage/Buildings			
Breezeway					Gardens/Landscaping			

INTERIOR

Open Concept					Efficient Kitchen Layout			
Master Bedroom					Ample Kitchen Storage			
Master Bedroom with Walk-in Closet					Ample Kitchen Work Surface			
Master Bathroom					Laundry Room			
Min. # of Bedrooms ____					Ampule Laundry Room Storage			
Bedroom Closet Space					Hardwood Floors			
Min. # of Bathrooms ____					Granite Countertops			
Ample Bathroom Storage Space					Finished Basement			
Min. # of Inside Storage Closets ____					Handicap Accessible			
Pantry					Mud Room			

NOTES

133

Head over to DirkWrites.com and sign up for the Inside Scoop! Receive a FREE copy of the How to Choose a House Checklist and a BONUS resource. Only those who sign up will find out what the BONUS is and how it can help you make better financial decision.

Notes:

_____

_____

_____

_____

_____

_____

_____

_____

_____

_____

_____

_____

_____

_____

_____

CHAPTER 20

Taking Care of Business

(Other Types of Insurance You Need or Need to Know About)

What is Insurance?

The *Oxford Dictionary* defines insurance as "An arrangement by which a company or the state undertakes to provide a guarantee of compensation for specified loss, damage, illness, or death in return for payment of a specified premium."

Life insurance is about income replacement so your family does not have to worry about how they are going to make ends meet without your income. Keep it simple and save money by choosing a term life insurance policy. If you have no one financially dependent on you, you really do not need life insurance.

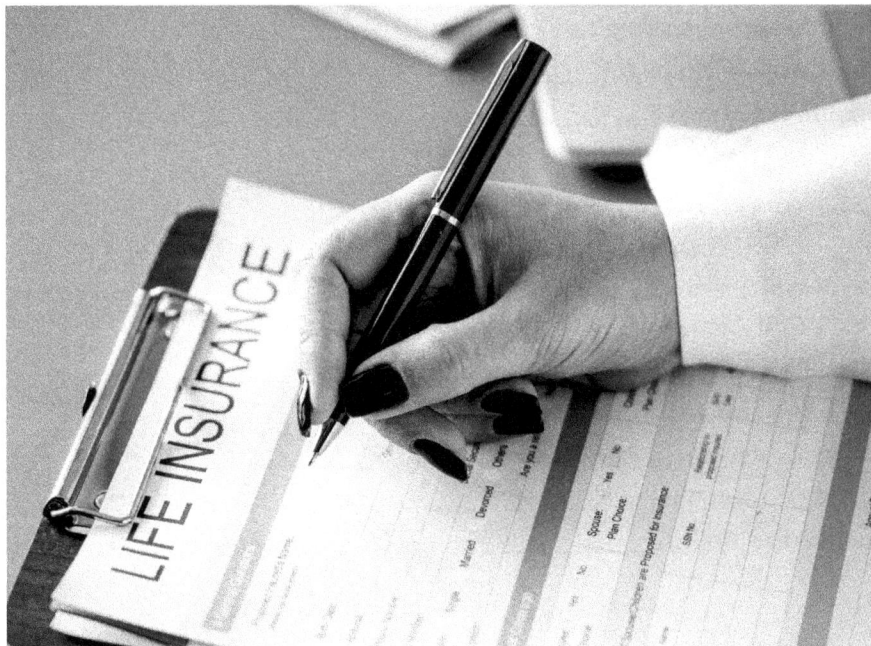

Do you need life insurance based on your family or dependent status? _____

Do you have life insurance now? _____

If you currently have life insurance, what type of life insurance do you have? _____

☐ **Term life insurance**
- Policy Start Date _____
- Policy Term _____
- Policy Coverage Amount $_____
- Premium Per Month $_____

☐ **Whole life insurance**
- Policy Start Date _____
- Current Policy Value $_____
- Current Cash Value $_____
- Have you taken out a loan against the policy? _____
- Do you still owe a balance on the loan? _____
- How much are you paying back each month? $_____
- Policy Coverage Amount $_____
- Premium Per Month $_____

☐ **Universal life insurance**
- Policy Start Date _____
- Current Policy Value $_____
- Current Cash Value $_____
- Have you taken a loan out against the policy? _____
- Do you still owe a balance on the loan? _____
- How much are you paying back each month? $_____
- Policy Coverage Amount $_____
- Premium Per Month $_____

☐ **Other** _____
- Policy Start Date _____
- Current Policy Value $_____
- Current Cash Value $_____
- Have you taken a loan out against the policy? _____
- Do you still owe a balance on the loan? _____
- How much are you paying back each month? $_____
- Policy Coverage Amount $_____
- Premium Per Month $_____

☐ **Other** _____

- Policy Start Date _____
- Current Policy Value $_____
- Current Cash Value $_____
- Have you taken a loan out against the policy? _____
- Do you still owe a balance on the loan? _____
- How much are you paying back each month? $_____
- Policy Coverage Amount $_____
- Premium Per Month $_____

Short-term disability (STD) and long-term disability (LTD) insurance are a must, as you have a 60%–80% chance of being disabled at some point during your working career.

Do you have short-term disability? _____

Do you have long-term disability? _____

Umbrella insurance is extra liability insurance that could be used after your home or auto policies have been exhausted. It's an added layer of protection that helps you keep more of what you have attained.

Do you have little or no debt? _____

Do you have assets or investments? _____

If you answered yes, you may need umbrella insurance to help protect what you have worked so hard to build. Contact your current insurance company to find out what the cost is for a $1,000,000 umbrella policy. You will also want to shop around as you did with your homeowners policy.

Long-Term care insurance is a policy that assists you outside of your medical coverage by covering daily needs. This type of insurance is not cheap. Start looking at this once you're nearing your mid to late 50s.

Longevity insurance is a policy that guarantees you a lifetime of income and typically starts paying you between ages of 80–85. However, your monthly payout will be determined by how much you originally deposited, when you made the deposit, and when you start to receive distributions.

You're not getting any younger, despite how you act. Thinking about your later years well in advance of arriving there is a good idea!

Notes:

_____

_____

_____

_____

_____

_____

_____

_____

_____

_____

_____

_____

CHAPTER 21

Start with
The End in Mind!
(Planning for Retirement and Investing)

It's easier and cheaper than ever to start saving for retirement, and the sooner you start, the sooner you can retire comfortably. How would you like to retire in your mid to late 40s, leaving you years and years to enjoy life, being able to do what you want, when you want? The opportunities are endless when you have that kind of financial freedom.

That sounds pretty awesome! Right?

Employer-sponsored retirement plans

Does your employer offer a retirement plan? _____

What type of retirement plan does your employer offer?

- ☐ **401(k)**
- ☐ **Roth 401(k)**
- ☐ **403(b)**
- ☐ **457**
- ☐ **Thrift Savings Plan (TSP)**
- ☐ **Blended Retirement System (BRS)**
- ☐ **SIMPLE IRA plan**
- ☐ **SEP IRA Plan**
- ☐ **Defined Benefit Plan**
- ☐ **Employee Stock Ownership Plan (ESOP)**
- ☐ **Money Purchase Plan**
- ☐ **Profit-Sharing**
- ☐ **Payroll Deduction IRA**
- ☐ **Other: _____**

Are you currently investing for retirement through your employer? _____

- *If so, what amount? $_____ per _____*

Do you plan to increase the amount you're investing for retirement? _____

- *If so, by what amount? $_____*

- *If so, when and how often? _____*

Does your employer offer a contribution matching plan of some kind? _____

- *If so, that's* free money *available to you. Are you going to take advantage of this?* _____

What kind of fees are associated with your employer's retirement plan? _____

Are you paying 1% or more in management fees? _____

If so, you may want to invest only up to the employer match. Otherwise, you will be paying more in fees and building less wealth compared to a low-cost investment plan.

Real Estate

Real estate can be invested both inside and outside of an employer sponsor retirement plan.

Do you have real estate as part of your portfolio? _____

What percentage do you have invested into real estate? _____

Dirk says . . .
TIME IS THE ULTIMATE EQUALIZER.

Non-Employer-Sponsored Retirement Options

Are you currently investing for retirement outside of an employer's plan? _____

- *If so, what amount? $_____ per _____*

Do you plan to increase the amount you're investing outside of your employer's plan? _____

- *If so, by what amount? $_____*

- *If so, when and how often?* _____

What form of non-employer-sponsored retirement investing are you using?
- ☐ Traditional IRA
- ☐ Roth IRA
- ☐ Spousal IRA
- ☐ Non-deductible IRA?

What kind of fees are associated with your non-employer retirement plan(s)?

_____

_____

_____

_____

_____

_____

_____

_____

Are you paying 1% or more in management fees? _____

If so, you may want to change to a low-cost investment or move your existing investments to a low-cost investment company. *Consult your investment advisor before making any changes as they could result in taxes and penalties.*

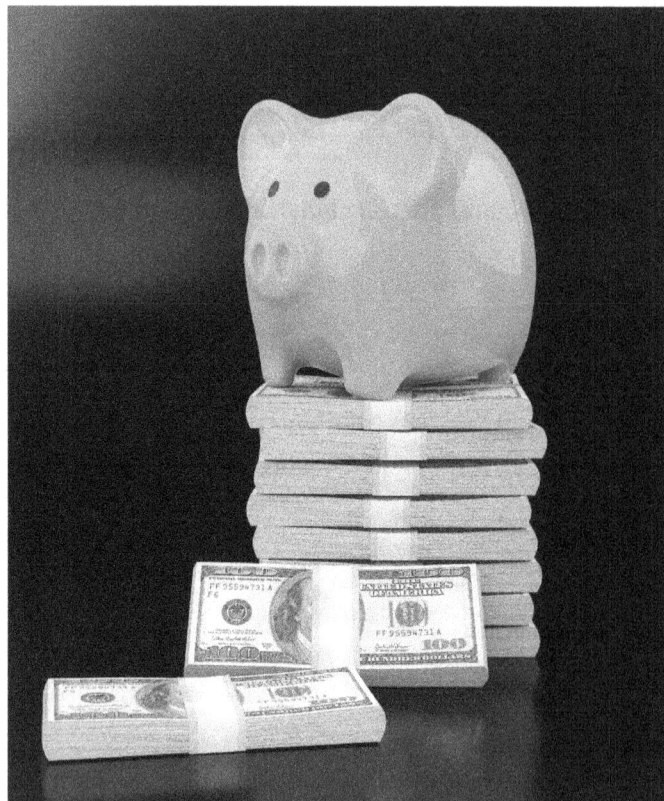

Non-Retirement Investing

Are you currently investing outside of employer and non-employer retirement plans? _____

- *If so, what amount? $_____ per _____*

Do you plan to increase the amount you're investing into your non-retirement portfolio? _____

- *If so, by what amount? $_____*

- *If so, when and how often? _____*

What is your financial goal of your nonretirement investing?

_____

_____

_____

_____

What kind of fees are associated with your non-employer retirement plan?

_____

_____

_____

_____

_____

Are you paying 1% or more in management fees? _____

If so, you may want to change to a low-cost investment or move your existing investments to a low-cost investment company. *Consult your investment advisor before making any changes, as they could result in taxes and penalties.*

Non-Retirement Savings

Are you currently saving money every month? _____

- *If so what amount? $_____ per _____*

Do you plan to increase the amount you're saving? _____

- *If so, by what amount? $_____*

- *If so, when and how often?* _____

What form of saving are you using?
- ☐ **Standard savings**
- ☐ **money market**
- ☐ **CD (certificate of deposit)**

Where are you putting your savings?

- ☐ **A traditional bank or credit union**
- ☐ **An online bank or credit union**

What interest rate are you being paid? _____

Are there minimums you must maintain to receive that interest rate? _____ $_____

Are you being charged a fee for falling below a minimum amount? _____ $_____

If so, how often have you fallen below the minimum amount? _____ $_____

If you have fallen below the minimum more than 3 times in the last 3 months, you need to change the type of account you have or move to a different financial institution. My vote is for you to move to a credit union.

Social Security

If you think you will be able to live on Social Security alone, you will be sadly mistaken and in a world of hurt going into your golden years. Your golden years are not the time you should have to worry about money. Right? Think of Social Security as an added bonus. It's nice to receive, but the amount will not be what you are expecting.

How much do you think you will receive in Social Security when you are eligible to receive it?

Annuity

In almost all cases, you should run away, far away, from anyone trying to sell you an annuity!

The only one you may want to look at is an immediate annuity. That's it! Otherwise, Run, Forrest, run!

Notes:

_____

_____

_____

_____

_____

_____

_____

_____

_____

_____

_____

_____

_____

CHAPTER 22

The Crossover

(Funerals and Burials)

WELL, ALL GOOD THINGS must come to an end. At some point, we are all going to die. This can be a difficult subject to bring up, let alone talk about or plan for in advance, but at some point, in the future, you will need to discuss your death and make decisions for that time in addition to writing your last will and testament. If you plan ahead, you can save yourself and your loved ones a lot of financial decisions at a very emotional time.

Have you talked with your family about your wishes surrounding your passing? _____

If not, what is holding you back?

_____

_____

_____

_____

Would you prefer a traditional funeral and burial? _____

Would you prefer a home funeral and burial? _____

Would you prefer to be embalmed? _____

Would you prefer to be cremated? _____

Would you prefer to donate your body to science? _____

Or would you prefer a combination of these choices? _____

Planning ahead will make it less stressful for your family during a time of sadness. It will also allow them to focus on being there for one another, not on making decisions about your funeral arrangements.

Notes:

_____

_____

_____

_____

_____

CHAPTER 23

Now What?
Your Definition of Financial
Success Revisited

YOU ARE ALMOST FINISHED with *The Quick-Start Guide to Financial Success Workbook*. Has your definition or vision of financial success changed? Do you need to change a few things? If not, that is great. If so, that is okay, too.

The next two pages are for you to revise your definition or vision of what financial success looks like to *you* now.

Current Date: _____

_____

_____

_____

_____

_____

_____

_____

_____

_____

_____

_____

_____

_____

_____

_____

_____

_____

_____

_____

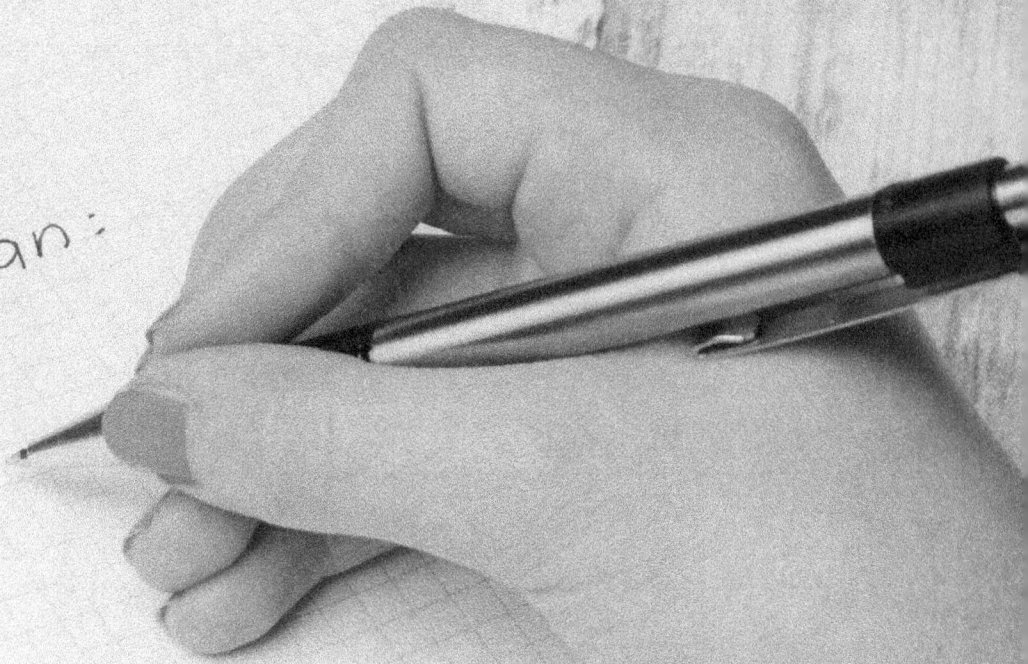

CHAPTER 24

What's Your Plan?

WHAT'S YOUR PLAN TO reach your definition or vision of financial success? Now that you have read *The Quick-Start Guide to Financial Success* and completed *The Quick-Start Guide to Financial Success Workbook* you have the basics down for changing your mindset, creating a budget, and making good financial decisions, you need a plan. What's yours?

The next two pages are for you to state your plan to get out of debt and reach your definition or vision of financial success. Make sure you review your plan on a regular basis to keep your plan in the forefront of your mind. Later you can always revisit your plan, and make changes as needed because it will change over time.

Current Date: _____

CONCLUSION

The Next Challenge

CONGRATULATIONS! YOU HAVE COMPLETED the workbook! The real test is being able to use the knowledge you have gained to make the changes needed to become financially successful.

When will you take your first step toward financial success?

WHY NOT START NOW?

YOU ARE WORTH IT!

**For more information and resources
from the book, visit:**

DirkWrites.com

P.S. – Don't forget to sign up for the Inside Scoop and receive a FREE copy of my budget and FREE copy of the How to Choose a House Checklist!

P.P.S. – I hope this workbook has helped you improve your financial situation in some way. I would be grateful if you would leave a review or comment so other people could benefit from your experience, insight, and impact on your life using this workbook.

Thanks again.

—Dirk

**Align your company's vision of success
by equipping everyone on your team
with a prosperity mindset.**

Contact Dirk for your next company event via:

DirkTalks.com